i fold with the hand i was dealt

poems

peter carlaftes

THREE ROOMS PRESS

NEW YORK CITY

i fold with the hand i was dealt

Cover and interior design:
KG Design International (katgeorges.com)

Cover photo: Wendy Fitz

First Edition

ISBN: 978-0-9884008-2-5

Published by
Three Rooms Press
New York, NY
threeroomspress.com

For Irene

contents

FOUR. Portable Papistry

FIVE. The I-Con Duit/Tuit

SIX. Confidence, Man

ONE:

i fold with
the hand
i was dealt

"There are some things one remembers even
though they may never have happened."

– Harold Pinter

run for your life

come
down
to
the den
– stepfather
and mom –

easy chair – plants

table lamp – between them

cigarets –
an ashtray – jar of
peanuts
between them

cushion
of suburbia: what
am I – eleven?
zenith
color console – ahead . . .

stepfather
thumbs
through the TV guide – stops
smirks
(stands) seems
pleasantly surprised
spins the dial (sits)

monotonous
american
let's
rip out
the wall – and
look at his tools

a show came on
called Run For Your Life

stepfather beamed
Here's your dreamboat Hon

this smug little ditty
drove mom to snap – The hell you say!
Who told you that?

stepfather (deflating)
sputtered – But
I thought you loved Ben Gazzara

while mother
denied
the passion
stepfather
presumed
I slid off the couch
and shuffled to bed
through a door
hung for wages
(thin-panelled failure)
time to grow up . . .

along
the way
I lived
below
some
other
troubled
two (when)
wisdom
spread over
the echoes
revising

what happened
that night
in the den – you see
mom held no torch
so
she got to thinking
just
who was this woman
(he) thought her to be
and
sure enough
when she left
he soon wed
another – well
images
run for your life.

I remember the day
he cut my hair
around
a plastic bowl

mom drew
hair back
on my head
with eyebrow
pencil strokes

be that as it may
beyond
nothing
belongs . . .

between each still

befores
find all

specious growth

part [one] boy

my first flight solo
came year seven – when
wide-eyed one noon
down Fordham
I wandered

three blocks later
a dark giant struck
pushing – Hey Boy
hardsqueeze
What You Got?

why me – well
back then there were
fake coins I collected
from a candy store:
toy worth redeemed
my lack of identity

so the giant up ahead
saw me traipsing along
unaware – made his play
for contents unknown:
that lump of pretend
bulging my pocket

growling – he cursed
each token until
one coin caught sun
end of game – all smile . . .

after the giant
lifted my quarter
and danced past a cop
like he owned the world
I've settled
where – others
can have it

part [two] man

time seventeen
ran me
dead city winter
up Fordham
arms flapping
to offset cold

steam heat – but
four blocks
bound shiver – till
up five flights
where
key'd fit door

when
(out of)
squad blue
prowling street
elsewise barren
jumped curb
pinning me
to front gate
of shoe store

the driver told me Kid
If You're Clean Don't Worry
his partner's translation –
Get In And Shut Up

inhabiting
a seat so warm
inaudibly
we tooled along
beneath the el-trains
shadowed tracks
pulled up outside

this social club:
hit the door – flanked
by law

instant he saw me
the barman lit up – like
ready to burst – Yeah
Him! That's The Guy

but split second later
he shook his head no
so the cop said
OK Kid
Now You Can Go

Go – fuming
Where? – cried
It's Forty Below!

brought safe, snug, warm
long short drive home
patent parting – Look Kid
Keep Your Nose Clean

I realized while climbing
my last flight of stairs
the sharpest tacks know
how to act like they care

+

took my guts
to the cleaners

oh, my – say
now
why do that
for
what
could
the cleaners . . .

well (perhaps)
whenever
there's will
but
the cleaners
were closed
so
me
and my guts
(then)
turned into
words

did I like my wife

we were more
need to be
numb – veiled
by love

– once –

evading
together
obliged

oh, what I won
while she slept
in the dark . . .

next stop hockshop
ticketstub please
insert your own strings
here

how many
pliant words
will it take
to resolve
this plural
did or didn't
when –
being

– once –

we were there
then
we weren't

even the drain leads somewhere

forever
ended
spiral

one pane
from the bottom

lost brother jazz
in a bottle
by the week

capsized mattress
– unkempt . . .

pulling
the ripcord,

(a woman)

we landed

a little bit west
of never to be . . .

deep inside that old trunk
in the corner of her room
lies an opalescent pin
in a red satin pouch

she wore it with the moon
on a night cupped crescent:
her finger circled
the amber stone

love – a yellow chair
dual in progress:
the water cools
our skin does not

merry dancing cattle
climbing to the slaughter
merry dancing cattle mount
a ladder without rungs

ends in fire – that
first kiss (burn)
soon to melt
reaching regardless

ends in fire: suite
madrigal (when)
in – love
was forever
again

the next to last wave

Shadow, Putt and I
play fetch along beach
surrounded by – an
endless blue
horizon

Shadow drops the stick
which I hurl back at sea
watching sand spin
through sun – gouging
wake-settled wave

Shadow strokes
between swells
snagging stick from swirl
and drops it where
my toes indent the sand

Putt wants the stick
and he's right
it's his turn
so I feign a hard throw
to get Shadow started
then toss the stick for Putt
at the safe shore-break . . .

This is what I do with my Death.

Death is the beach, two dogs and me.

The weather's always fair, so we splash
in the surf.

We experience no hunger or thirst.

The sun never sets and we never grow tired.

Death is constant. Only sand, sea and horizon.

I tell the dogs anything. We're old friends.

They cannot talk, but we are here.

Shadow is a black lab; 11 years old
when I put her to sleep. Tumors set in
and she had lost the will to live. I remember
when her eyes turned stone-grey from the
syringe full of Sodium Pentothal and I
believe her last thought is what
brings us together now.

Putt-Putt is a long-haired dachshund
terrier mix who lived 17 years.

Nothing changes inhabiting eternity.

The dogs and I are as we were
in our prime.

The babies are in their first trimester.

The three fetuses I chose to abort while alive
dangle from umbilical cords
attached to my body.

I interpret these appendages to be
the selfless tenor of death:

others carried the pain of loss in life
so it's up to me to carry
these inchoate souls forever

excuse me
the dogs are
wagging their tails

we're going to walk
down the beach
now

TWO:

the i can't-o cantos

"... What shall I do?
I shall rush out as I am
and walk the streets..."
— *T.S. Eliot*

i.
blueprint

structure
success

the road
most taken

after
many
violations
I evolved
without
dispassion

later on
I'll drop dead
without pockets

ii.
foundation

reality
throws a right

lays you down
on the canvas

towel toss
time

the rules
make
us broken

iii.
spitting image

first time
flat out

foot to floor
(bored)

seeing hope
headlong

until you find
the rear-view
mirror

iv.
so they killed
us already

one click – Kaboom
through the chamber

fragments
meant
to love
other
fragments

dug out of
the same dead face
that will never be
what could've been

v.
or lack
thereof

each day leaves us
with dreams
less focused

no one comes
prepared

no one leaves
in acceptance

if you can find
more than
a moment
in this life

then
you can afford
to fly me there
and I will be
your friend

vi.
small world

bloodlines
may dictate
you conquer
a village

desire
nothing left

buy what they say
when they say

you can't
run as fast
as them

vii.
standstill

act lost
and smile

hide it well
the check will clear

hang
a price tag
on the wall

someone
will purchase
the moment
you gave up

viii.
salad days

the sound of own voice
can be cut fresh daily
behind eyelids
which dangle
soft words
re-imagined
as dreams
peel away
exposing

the never ending caravan
of your blessed mistakes

ix.
hard on the vine

we become produce
for consumers
such as loneliness
and love

torn creatures
destined
for the compost
heap cycle

interns of dust
until forever
remains

x.
between sleep

playground
regrets

as sunset
darkens

kind fields
beckon
from
either side

the days
rewound

dissolve
unfettered

lying down
just
one more
time

Nothing Ever Happened

We were all put here
two seconds ago

I know it!
the past
isn't real

all history's
been created
by some
genius
super-hacker
from the – um
. . . well,
I wasn't implanted
with that information
But
This Earth
We only Think
we're on this planet
spinning around

some deep, dark
galaxy
when in reality
this place is just
a big computer screen
and some slick being's
having quite a time

great imagination
you've got to admit

creating names
like – Genghis Khan,
Sacco and Vanzetti,
or Anna May Wong
for that matter – hell

I didn't even write
this piece

how the hell
do I know this?

THREE:

P   N - Y

E   E

D I G R E

O   E

P - R   D

Pandarin Orange

under moon-lit distant yore
(circa: seventh dynasty)
clever pimp coin noble pun
stealing fruit off neighbor's tree

that
render – smile
even still

however – which
require
will

for dream – procuring
sacred brothel
Hop Yu Ho's Retreat

would fill no more
than pipe without
much-needed
currency

so hop pimp quick
first house of Jade
where threat of death
ill-get her gains

next stop on list
find Lotus – whom
learn tighter grip
make lip fat soon

achieving goal
round four a.m.
pimp enter Ho's
by coin in hand

from point of sale
to first crack dawn
marquee repainted
"Pandarin Orange"

while name imply
most carnal place
for wanton lust
'pon shanghaied waif

pimp – shake girls down
to kick back graft
thus, short-run – soon
joy house full-packed

moral of endeavor:

idea – good;
but action better

(although)
sitting duck
leave little room
for error

else – watch rear

(seeing) rival
Wing-Ding brothel
burn same year

Señor Catapult

'twas myriad agos – therein
the heart of old Madrid
came born a nut-brown boy
(about) the same time as El Cid

(as story goes)
some moments later – though

abiding poor but honest
often-gauged if whether kin,
would cut him any much above
else sticks short, bitter end;

made thus far Sixto Juan Jimenez – well

where ill-off found fifteen
enduring first cruel night alone
he tripped mid-flight unseen
across this half-cocked catapult

left to rot ditched roadside – so

while pain diverted hunger
likewise lame with dawn arose
to scavenge nearby fields perchance
for each part lie hid whole

in lieu of shagging ass back home – then

once search net tools of trade
he completed work by noon
and swapped first hand who bit
for five goats and two doubloons;

at which time secondhand struck – soon

after goats fetched horse and cart
he promptly opened namesake shop
where escalating arms nonstop
begat the first used weapon lot

and yet so sad to say
dreadful few stood side his grave
being most were (on that day)
at de Gamma's big parade

Forethought the Aftertaste

while meantime's rife
with good intent
just ponder this
most provident gent

whose live-let life
held dear by all
so far back – hence
I can't recall

save notion now
need reckon when:
why even death
was kind to him

though a subsequent gene
matter-fact did in turn
help mid warm night – conceive
part of Adolf Hitler

or was it
Adolphe Menjou . . .

I can't remember
exactly

Sir Realist

anew – war was stirring

so valiant
Sir Realist
donned armor again

though once sheathed in metal
all fight in him left

resigning, knight errant
conceived his own death

he set off afoot
for the same battlefield
where most of his
cohorts had died

then dug out a grave
and lay down inside
with his trusty crossbow
there – awaiting
who first happened by

a portly knave
so foul of smell
that barely
could our hero
keep stock-still
while
fetid wretch
unfurled the scroll
the gallant knight
had written
and left beside hole

(which
began)

Herein Lies Sir Realist
Who Died On This Spot
Please Cover This Grave – His –
None Braver of Heart

but the reeking louse
grumbled
Can't Read

cried Enough
did Sir Realist
and fired his bow
directly through forehead
of noisome old rogue
and covered him quickly
to smother the stench
which hero thought worse than
tramp's soon rotting flesh

posturing
that rogue is now dead
due to being ill-bred
though more thoughtful a plan
would have me there instead

so when valorous knight
mounted scalawags mare
his desire to fight had
returned beyond pale

and while crossing this field
where so many were lost
he appraised their revenge
at immeasurable cost

as he pledged to his flag
and then yanked the reigns hard
on to train men to kill
for King, Country and God

FOUR:

PORTABLE PAPISTRY

calendar christ

say

*

check-out
that sweet dish
tacked -unclad
to cross

*   *

miss
led-on
by format
beholden
to us

*

no doubt
she meant well
(great set 'a jugs)

†

not to mention
what beautiful
nails

chicken
shit christ

arise in the ring – now
ya cheek-turning bum

let hallowed be rematch
ye – shall overcome

and – since, first ascent
left you second to none

all here, still await thee
tied – minus one

citizen
christ

his feet are nailed together
through a pop-up footrest

his palms are pinned flat
facing plush velvet arms

another day
huh jeez

christ
not again

fell asleep
watching t-v

a   m   e   n

Down to Earth

by virtue – once sixfold
determined mid-Sabbath
commanding his agent
Ordain Open-Planet . . .

where given deemed Thy realm anew
found teeming plenty-proud until
that misanthropic legion known
as patronage arrived . . .

thus too soon 'side buffet bode acquittance
when Maury's first stone vested least-line resistance
Who Do I Tithe For Another Eclipse – well
God advised Maury, Thou'd Best See The Light
yet Maury – squinched Not If It's Burning My Eyes
so God vouched Me-Willing, The Sun Also Drops
but Maury broke beeline – off His-speed to bar . . .

then up next Cliff – with gladhand – swooned
That Stud In Your Garden, Oh! Fly Me To The Moon – 'Cept
One Little Thing (Cliff stopped stroking God's hand)
I Was Swirling My – Feet 'Round This Nasty Old Creek
And Look At These – Wrinkles You Almighty Beast
Why Let Alone – Witness They're Still Soaking Wet
So Hate To Prod Thou Make Good – But
Purge This Foul Liquid – Or Least Heat It Up
only – God welshed defraying My Red Sea's A Blast –
to which 'bout-turned Cliff seething Snake In The Grass . . .

here Sadie slighted Sam-in-tow
approaching misty-eyed although
since Sammy hustled galaxies
from stunning SuperNova – he
stood aloof while Sadie cooed
Earth Consecrates Thy Magnitude – then
Sammy surged You-Damn Good Show

That Rib Thing Was Tremendous – though
What's With All This Fruit?
Now – Don't Get Me Wrong
I Mean – Apples Are Great
And I Love Bananas
But Who Would "Eat" This Kiwi Crap?
And You-Forbid Why Pomegranates
Now God – If I Were You –
But Sadie tugged his coat sleeve pointing
Look – There's Hal And Doris Hon
So – off in Sadie's wake through crowd
went Sammy stirring Bah God-Schmod . . .

what 'ponward streak swept 'hind repose
wore other cheek pale 'yond because
cutting-swarth 'mongst doubtage found
none-but-The-Big-Bang nigh-due-Thee-now and
no one took this guy in vain seeing how as deftly,
The Big Bang prefattened-calf such proceeding
Thou Clever God – Given Thy Rush –
Yet Why Assuage Thine-Own-sends With
Come Judgement-Day Exemption – If
The Concept But To Appease Your
Lust For Their Idolatry – Sir, thus
The Big Bang spoke

where light years removed
the nearest, black hole
hiding face between hands
God – desperately moaned
What Am I Going
To Do – Do
So –
here's
what He did
back at His
studio . . .

spitting out, the bitterness
dove headlong into work
eliminating pomegranates
from all future endeavors

but – after years of toil – Had
unveiled two more offcasts
He saw that pleasing others
was a misbegotten task – so

God decided to inhabit his masterpiece

He gave up his immortality
and took the place of a fetus
carried by Irene Botswain
in Clear Lake, Iowa

On January 7th, 1935, God was born Jerry Botswain

God [Jerry] made it up through the minor leagues and,
in 1958, played second base for the Cleveland Indians

On February 3rd, 1959, while God [Jerry] visited his parents
the plane carrying Buddy Holly, Richie Valens and The Big Bopper
slammed into the family's home, killing everyone instantly

although but in substance,
God's work will live on
and that's why the desire
to create exists in anyone

FIVE:

The I-Con Duit/Tuit

"Whatever you touch and believe in today
is going to be illusion – tomorrow . . ."
– Luigi Pirandello

Little Did We Know

While sitting in
The Algonquin
Me and George
devised a plan
to help the world
heal old wounds

—so—

we set off from
New York
and built a church
in north Tehran

—but—

upon our work's completion
their army tore it down
so all roads led us home
where bitter tasting
was defeat

—well—

our
first
impulse
was

Hey
Let's Destroy A Mosque

—and—

believe you
Me and George

put the word
out on the street
that we were in
the market for
some serious
explosives

—but—

the only people
we found selling
were the ones
inside the mosque

—so—

while we saw
much irony
inside the situation
our failure stemmed
from thinking
we could change
mankind's direction

—and—

even though
Me and George
began with best intentions
not all ideas are worthy

lest one find themselves
between
the horns of a dilemma

The Eventual Embrace
of Virtual Reality

I'm about to explode
sitting bumper to bumper

Rachmaninoff isn't doing it

I need a shot of phone-in talk show

This is Freddie Suborn
You're on the air, America

Yeah, Freddie, I'm Doug

Hello, Doug

Hello yourself
Last week you hung up on my 6-year-old daughter
You rat bastard
She was so excited to speak to you
and you hung up before she could say two words
If I ever get my hands on you
I'll beat your face to a pulp

Let me tell you, Doug,
anything you do to my face
would be an improvement
and there can't be much hope
for your precious little daughter
with a macho jerk
like you for a father

This is Freddie Suborn
You're on the air, America
Hello, Freddie
I'm Elizabeth

Hello, Elizabeth

You probably don't remember, Freddie
but about 12 years ago
we went out on a date
and you couldn't get it up
Freddie couldn't get it up
Freddie couldn't . . .

This is Freddie Suborn
I don't know that woman
I don't know anyone named Elizabeth Lonnigan
You people out there by your phones
listen to me
This is not the Stomp On Freddie Show
I'm here to exchange ideas
with people who care about
making this a better world

You're on the air, America

Hello, Freddie, I'm Chuck

Hello, Chuck

I was 30 years with the power company
and I'm retired now, Freddie
I don't have many interesting thoughts
but, this morning
I read a thing in the paper about Virtual Reality
and I got to thinking that Virtual Reality
would be a good solution
for the homeless problem

What do you mean by that, Chuck?

Well, if you put these Virtual Reality chips
into the heads of the homeless
then they'd think
that their stomachs were full
and they'd quit bothering
the hardworking people

That's an interesting idea, Chuck
But what are we going to do with these vagrants
when they drop dead from starvation –
What are we going to do with their bodies, Chuck?

I don't think it would be too hard
to build some cubicles for them
somewhere out of the way, Freddie

What about nourishment, Chuck?

I'm coming to that part, Fred
So you put the homeless people in cubicles
and you hook 'em all up to a vat of protein
then you get high school drop outs
to clean bedpans for minimum wage
that way
you're keeping the homeless off the streets
and you're keeping the kids from selling drugs
Now my kids are all grown, Freddie,
but I don"t want my grandchildren
to walk down these streets
the way they are now
you know what I mean

Yes I do, Chuck
I think it's a terrific idea
Personally
I'd jump at the chance to give my tax dollars
to a program like yours
Let's all write a letter to the president
Thanks, Chuck

Shaking my head
I look to my left
and see a well-dressed woman
in a two-toned Mercedes
talking to a cellular phone

Personally
I'd jump at the chance to place her in a Virtual Reality
where she only believed she was talking on the phone
then I'd just leave her in the weeds
by the side of the road
and sell her car
to feed the homeless
for a whole damned calendar year

I'll write a letter
when I get home

if I ever get home

There's nothing worse than being stuck in traffic . . .

I'm a Victim of
the Products
of My Time

This is the story
of what happened
to me
last time
in Las Vegas
see/when
I bought one of those
silly cocktails
with the spinning, white lights
in the base of the cup and
went into the john to piss,
my pee came out a stream of
spinning, white lights
(then)
the guy next to me
started screaming,
Look! Look!
and when a crowd
formed around me
asking,
Where did you get That?
I just pointed
a direction
Over There
and the herd
stampeded – off
in that
very same direction

many
were trampled;
women and children
first

(then/soon)
others were peeing
spinning, white lights – so
I strutted back
to my room
head high
proud
to help preserve
"the"
American Way – of
accumulating more
albeit/from
the waste
which
we expel
but/then
I had to shit
and when I wiped
my ass
I saw
a bright, blue
stripe
around
my turd – so
I ran out in the hall
to incite
another movement

(but)
the empty hall
of quiet air
stood empty
(up/until)
some kid
two doors down
pushed his
food cart out
(then/puked)
a dark, red splash
from which came
these rosy jumping chunks
kind of
like those funny
beans – that
just went
bouncing
down the hall
across
the greenish
speckled carpet
as we both
(stood/in)
amazement
(there)
admiring
the nature of
American invention

so
(strong/still)
in the face
of great recession
.   .   .

bright red
bouncing chunks,

white-lit
(pee/and)
blue-striped
shit

what a land of
brave and free
. . .

only
trouble is
(I've/been)
afraid
to jack off
ever since

Equal
Wrongs

in the very near future
of
forever
comes this:
Single Mother/Painter
and
Performer
Maya Stroh
sues Dade County,
Florida
(for)
Half-a-Billion
Bucks
. . .

Yes

.

Half-a-Billion
Bucks
. . .

Why?

here
the story
goes
. . .

starts
in Pittsburg,
Pennsylvania
. . .

she's
a painter:
Maya Stroh;
likes acrylics;
there
impoverished;
soon
with child
then
abandoned
by a deadbeat
'midst
one winter – caked
with snow
. . .

Stroh,
Maya
gave
birth to a boy
named Jackson
who
cried all the time
except – feeding
which
made painting
kind of hard
but – she
kept at it
until
one day
after feeding
baby
Jackson
shot some puke
across
her painting
and

while
creamy 'lixer
trickled down
the canvass
more stars
were dreamt
there
begat – a
universe

. . .

Jackson Colic
coined
the mother
and
she
took it on
the road

. . .

fed the baby
Topless
as
she painted
on the stage

. . .

found success
in
North
Miami Beach

. . .

Four Nights
a week

. . .

Jackson Colic
8 PM
and
even though
the audience
consisted
mainly of
local men – who
seemed to get a charge
eyeing Maya's
breasts –
Ms. Stroh
was now
successful
on a stage
creating art
and
her art began
to sell
. . .

then
along came
Child Services
of
Dade County,
Florida
to
remove
the baby
Jackson
from
the custody
of Stroh
claiming
the baby's
well-being
wasn't

then
as the mother
fought
the court
for her right
to nurture,
little Jackson
passed away
from
what some said
a broken heart:
he missed
the limelight

. . .

so
on the Supreme
Court docket – came
Stroh V. Dade
for
half-a-billion bucks
only
now/then
the paintings
little Jackson
helped create
held 10 million dollar
starting bids
at Sotheby's South

. . .

– But

. . .

Our
Time
alluding to
the words on
this page
. . .

Our
Time
. . .

Our
Time
. . .

Our
Time – is

U
p
.

SIX:

Confidence, Man

"La vida es una mierda – muchas veces huele bien."

"Life is shit – that eventually smells good."

– Peter Carlaftes

Remembering
Dippity-Do

women would use
the product
to roll up their hair
in curlers
then open cans
and slave
over stove:

with a white filter
dangling
from the corner
of her mouth
the wife laughs
as a long ash
falls off into
tuna surprise

and hubby
sitting
at formica
laughs too
while lighting
own with zippo
bought in Seoul

telling kids
who run in
to pipe down

and John
was dead
but not
Martin
or Bobby

and not
quite Tet
(not yet)

and
the TV set is
on the blink

and the repairman
replaces a tube

and
then
Zap – June 8th
appears upon
the screen

and the repairman
sighs
That's My Birthday . . .

the first day drawn
in the military draft

and everybody
stared directly
at the set
whose brand
was Zenith
as Chet Huntley
started speaking
of equality on Earth

but
there
couldn't be
equality
if the family next door
bought a bigger
better car

though
the bodies
came home
equally dead

and the repairman
got paid
driving off
in a daze

while the family
bowed their heads
and the youngest
started grace
over plates
full of tuna
surprise

Which Land is Mine

got thrown off a Trailways bus
trying to
hide behind my seat

somber driver told me that
Nobody Rides For Free

started walking
through a city
darkness falling
crossed a bridge

came across
convenience store
where clerk stood
all alone

moseyed up
to counter
posing
What Would You Think
About Splitting The Till
Then Saying That Two Guys
Robbed You With A Shotgun

his answer was
I Wouldn't

ran me
out of store
and – soon
ideas

when a Tim's Donuts van
pulled up along curb

so I made
myself
a sight unseen
while driver
took a tray
inside

snuck around his van
while he shot the breeze
with clerk

turning
handle
opened

took a trayful
for myself

disappeared
behind store
through the backside
of apartments
and undid the latch
of somebody's patio

rested on a chaise
eating donut after donut
all the while waiting for
the sound of sliding door
then maybe bullets
or a siren
but the silence
stayed my friend

pondering
my future
beyond
the chaise

was grim
so I quit there
while ahead
deciding
here I do belong

took the path
that none had taken

found a bag
on the grounds
and loaded it
with donuts

walking midnight
through the dawn
dreaming
what the world
could be

stuck my thumb at
sight of sun
and some salesman
stopped his car

asked me
Where Abouts You Going?

answered
Far As You Can
Take Me

we drove off
heading south

he reached
toward his pocket
perhaps for a gun
or to unzip his fly
but his hand held
Want A Smoke?

smiling
Yeah
popped my bag
Want A Donut?

Least Inconsequential

once upon
that only once
one spends a day
of life –

I lived in Houston
and sold Huggies:
those round, foam sleeves
that keep beer cold

Houston – was
the perfect place
for Huggies

Clearview
East
even more so

where the liquor store
looked grander
than the church
across the street

abutting channel
kids hunched over
doing something
having fun

fought my way over
through pure, wet heat

found them
dropping trash
into the muck

I asked them
What You Doing?

they all chimed
Breaking Through The Sludge

I looked down the wall
at the coat of black oil
and the pile they'd built
out of cigaret butts
and candy bar wrappers
just piled up – stable

not heavy enough
to break through

one kid dropped a rock
Ker-Ploop – pile gone
then yelled – Hey
Let's Go To Kenny's
And Dig Up Worms

another kid moaned
You Can Only
Dig Worms
In The Morning

then a pale
long-faced man
came out of
the store
with a pint
in a brown
paper bag
and a whistle
C'mon!
Let's Go, T.C.

one boy waved
See You At
Sunday School
on Saturday

T.C. waved back
asking his dad
Is It True
You Can Only
Catch Worms
In The Morning?

his dad spit
a brown stream
of juice out
and said
Ain't No Need
To Know Nothin'
'Bout Worms

as the kids
crossed a bridge
into heat
something blurred

through the window
of the store
I could see
the owner's smile
as I carried in
ten boxes
of two dozen
Huggies

he cleared off
space for one
and put
the others
in the back
paid me cash
100 dollars

said he'd call
and nodded
Thanks

backing out on
main street – saw
the church's
marquee read
Sunday School
Every Saturday
At 10:30 AM

then
stuck inside the loop
with many others
I envisaged
my future

we can only take
but so much weight
till everyone must fall

and win or lose
won't matter

for now
keeping cool
and warm

+

Check and Mate

all you can do
from now – forward
is wait
so
there I was
– waiting –

just peeked
behind curtain
and there – it
(Death)
was

down on
the street
with
scepter,
dark cape
and a
cavernous
cowl

while
each store
he passes
becomes
boarded
remains

looks
like
that cat
playing chess
in the film

hear
his
hard step
hit the stair

precious
seconds
to prepare
my absurd
scheme

quickly
grabbing
frozen sperm
and embryo
I stand beside
front door
which silently
swings open
with pyrotechnic
swirl

enter Death
(surprisingly
about
same height
as me)
bellowing
from the depth
Your Time's Up

well,
with that
same, slim
chance
enabling
each of our
beginnings
I aim for
Death's loin
wielding
procreative
means

Death scoffs
warning
It's All Been
Tried Before
but I sense
something
changing

a disconnected
self-involvement

Death just
traipses
out the door

an original
thought,
such pure
inspiration

blindsiding
old Beez
through
insemination

now – at a loss

what to do
with
success
because
down on
the street
I know of
no place
to go – so
I start
searching
for Death

first
Carmine
then Leroy
Cornelia
and Jones,
all boarded-up
empty
in pitch-black
erode

when
straight up
past 7th
near Bleecker
and Grove
no doubt
caught tail-end
of preoccupied
robe

I've spent a lifetime
where others could
care less if I lived

should I follow
on Death's heel?

not a
blueprint
or map

– methinks –

I'll take a chance
and create
my own path

PETER CARLAFTES is a New York-based
poet, playwright and performer. His books
include *A Year on Facebook* (humor), *Drunkyard
Dog* (poetry) and *Triumph for Rent* (3 plays).

With this collection, Carlaftes throws in the
hand he was dealt and creates a brand new
deck of cards.

books on three rooms press

POETRY

Hala Alyan
Atrium

Peter Carlaftes
DrunkYard Dog
I Fold with the Hand I Was Dealt

Joie Cook
When Night Salutes the Dawn

Thomas Fucaloro
Inheriting Craziness is Like
  a Soft Halo of Light

Patrizia Gattaceca
Soul Island

Kat Georges
Our Lady of the Hunger
Punk Rock Journal

Robert Gibbons
Close to the Tree

Karen Hildebrand
One Foot Out the Door
Take a Shot at Love

Matthew Hupert
Ism is a Retrovirus

Dominique Lowell
Sit Yr Ass Down or You Ain't gettin
  no Burger King

Jane Ormerod
Recreational Vehicles on Fire
Welcome to the Museum of Cattle

Susan Scutti
We Are Related

Jackie Sheeler
to[o] long

The Bass Player from Hand Job
Splitting Hairs

Angelo Verga
Praise for What Remains

George Wallace
Poppin' Johnny
EOS: Abductor of Men

PHOTOGRAPHY-MEMOIR

Mike Watt
On & Off Bass

FICTION

Michael T. Fournier
Hidden Wheel

DADA

Maintenant: Journal of
Contemporary Dada Art & Literature
(Annual poetry/art journal, since 2003)

SHORT STORIES

Have a NYC: New York Short Stories
Annual Short Fiction Anthology

HUMOR

Peter Carlaftes
A Year on Facebook

PLAYS

Madeline Artenberg &
Karen Hildebrand
The Old In-and-Out

Peter Carlaftes
Triumph For Rent (3 Plays)
Teatrophy (3 More Plays)

Larry Myers
Mary Anderson's Encore
Twitter Theater

TRANSLATIONS

Patrizia Gattaceca
Isula d'Anima / Soul Island
(poems in Corsican with
English translations)

George Wallace
EOS: Abductor of Men (American
poems with Greek translations)

three rooms press | new york, ny
current catalog: www.threeroomspress.com